FAST CARS

dodge
VIPER

by Jameson Anderson

Reading Consultant:
Barbara J. Fox
Reading Specialist
North Carolina State University

Content Consultant:
Paul Hayes
Viper Club of America
Minnesota Chapter

Capstone
press

Mankato, Minnesota

Blazers is published by Capstone Press,
151 Good Counsel Drive, P.O. Box 669, Mankato, Minnesota 56002.
www.capstonepress.com

Library of Congress Cataloging-in-Publication Data
Anderson, Jameson.
    Dodge Viper / by Jameson Anderson.
    p. cm. — (Blazers. Fast cars)
    Summary: "Simple text and colorful photographs describe the history and
models of the Dodge Viper" — Provided by publisher.
    Includes bibliographical references and index.
    ISBN-13: 978-1-4296-1278-4 (hardcover)
    ISBN-10: 1-4296-1278-9 (hardcover)
    1. Viper automobile — Juvenile literature. I. Title. II. Series.
TL215.V544A54 2008
629.222'2 — dc22   2007033124

Editorial Credits
Angie Kaelberer, editor; Bobbi J. Wyss, designer; Jo Miller, photo researcher

Photo Credits
Alamy/Transtock Inc., 22
AP Images/Richard Sheinwald, 7
Corbis/Bettmann, 8, 14
Getty Images Inc./AFP/Jeff Haynes, 15 (bottom right), 29
Ron Kimball Stock/Ron Kimball, cover, 5, 6, 11 (both), 12, 15 (top and bottom
    left), 17, 19, 26–27
Shutterstock/JD, 10; Michael Stokes, 20–21
ZUMA Press/Alan Look/Icon SMI, 24

Essential content terms are **bold** and are defined at the bottom of the page
where they first appear.

1 2 3 4 5 6 13 12 11 10 09 08

TABLE OF CONTENTS

Meet the Snake 4

Viper History 9

Viper's Quick Strike 16

Viper Features 23

Looking Ahead 28

Timeline 14

Diagram 26

Glossary 30

Read More 31

Internet Sites 31

Index 32

chapter 1

MEET THE SNAKE

A sleek Dodge Viper speeds around the highway's curves. Everyone who sees it whiz by wishes they could be in the driver's seat.

Dodge first sold Vipers in 1992. The cars were built to be fast and powerful. They are like the muscle cars of the 1960s and 1970s.

1992 Viper RT/10

Some 1996 models had yellow wheels.

fast fact

Vipers are named after the fast and dangerous viper snake.

Viper concept car

chapter 2

VIPER HISTORY

Dodge built the first Viper *concept car* in 1989. Engineers spent three years making the car. The first Vipers had no roof.

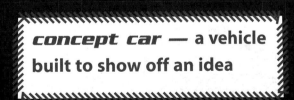

concept car — a vehicle built to show off an idea

The first Vipers were red. By
1996, buyers could get Vipers
in bright blue, black, deep yellow,
and other colors.

1996 Viper RT/10

In 1996, Dodge improved
the Viper. The new GTS
and the improved RT/10
models had more engine
power than earlier Vipers.

fast fact

Dodge engineers studied the Lamborghini sports
car before building the Viper's V10 engine.

VIPER TIMELINE

The Viper is introduced at the Detroit Auto Show.

The Viper is available in black, yellow, and green.

1990

1994

1992

Buyers snap up the first Vipers off the assembly line.

Dodge shows off the
Viper GTS coupe.

1996

The new RT/10 produces
450 horsepower.

1997

1996

2003

Dodge improves the RT/10.

Dodge introduces the
newest Viper, the SRT-10.

chapter 3

VIPER'S QUICK STRIKE

Powerful engines make Vipers among the fastest cars on the road. The SRT-10 engine pumps out 600 *horsepower*.

horsepower — a unit for measuring an engine's power

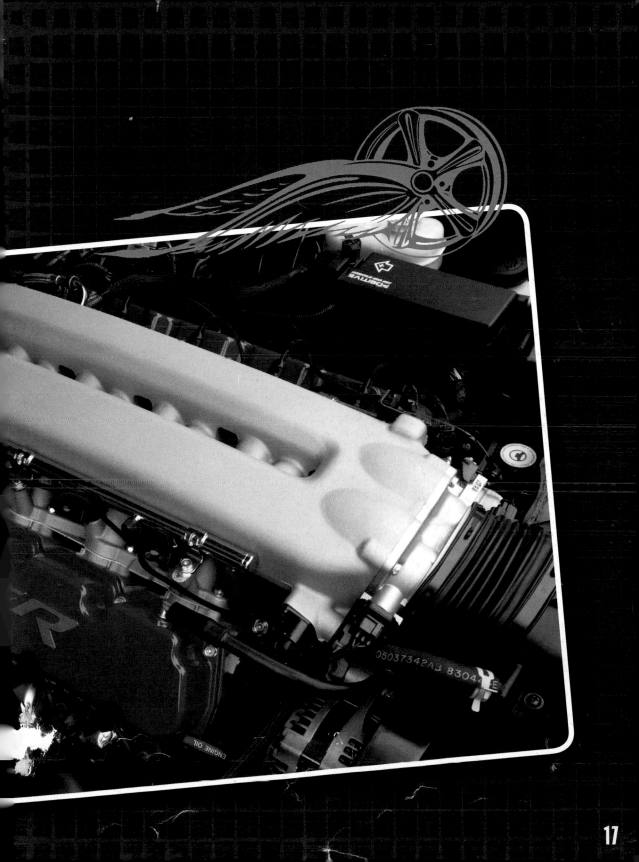

Vipers reach top speeds of about 170 miles (274 km) per hour. The SRT-10 zips from zero to 60 miles (97 km) per hour in less than four seconds.

To make the Viper faster, the body is made of a lightweight plastic. The plastic is called resin transfer molding.

chapter 4

VIPER FEATURES

To start Vipers, drivers push a red button on the *dashboard*. Many race cars also have push-button starters.

dashboard — a panel on the interior of a car that contains the instruments and controls

The first Vipers had no door handles on the outside. Today's Vipers have a small push-button door handle.

fast fact

In the 1990s, the TV show *Viper* featured a Viper that changed into a crime-fighting vehicle.

VIPER DIAGRAM

air scoop

headlight

grille

spoiler

aluminum wheel

chapter 5

LOOKING AHEAD

The 2008 SRT-10 is the most powerful Viper yet. Can future Vipers push the limits of speed even farther?

fast fact

Dodge showed off the 675-horsepower Mopar Viper Coupe concept car in 2007.

2008 Viper SRT-10

GLOSSARY

concept car (KON-sept KAR) — a vehicle built to show off an idea

dashboard (DASH-bord) — a panel on the front interior of a car that contains the instruments and controls

engineer (en-juh-NIHR) — someone who designs and builds machines, vehicles, or other structures

horsepower (HORSS-pou-ur) — a unit for measuring an engine's power

Lamborghini (Lam-bore-GHEE-nee) — a sports car built in Italy

model (MOD-uhl) — a specific type of car

sleek (SLEEK) — smooth and shiny

READ MORE

Doeden, Matt. *Sports Cars.* Horsepower. Mankato, Minn.: Capstone Press, 2005.

Hawley, Rebecca. *Viper.* Superfast Cars. New York: PowerKids Press, 2007.

Maurer, Tracy. *Viper.* Full Throttle. Vero Beach, Fla.: Rourke, 2007.

INTERNET SITES

FactHound offers a safe, fun way to find Internet sites related to this book. All of the sites on FactHound have been researched by our staff.

Here's how:
1. Visit *www.facthound.com*
2. Choose your grade level.
3. Type in this special code **1429612789** for age-appropriate sites. You may also browse subjects by clicking on letters, or by clicking on pictures or words.
4. Click on the **Fetch It** button.

FactHound will fetch the best sites for you!

www.FACTHOUND.com

INDEX

colors, 10, 14
concept cars, 9, 28
    Mopar Viper Coupe,
      28

engines, 13, 16
engineers, 9, 13

horsepower, 15, 16, 28

interior features
    dashboard, 23
    push-button starters,
      23

Lamborghini, 13

models
    GTS, 13, 15
    RT/10, 13, 15
    SRT-10, 15, 16, 18, 28

push-button door
    handles, 25

race cars, 23
resin transfer molding,
    20

speed, 18, 28
sports cars, 13